180 Mornings About Me

Grades 3-6

SHEILA GARTH

1. ABOUT ME

2. FEELINGS & THINGS

3. WOULD YOU RATHER

4. CREATE

5. ADD TO...

Little Friends for Big Feelings

Copyright © 2025 Moodamals

All rights reserved. No part of this publication may be reproduced, distributed, or transmitted in any form or by any means without the prior written permission of the publisher, except in the case of brief quotations in critical reviews and certain other non-commercial uses permitted by copyright law.

Editing by KarolynEditsBooks.com

ISBN 979-8-9923349-0-6

https://www.moodamals.com

Welcome to 180 Mornings About Me!

This workbook is designed to help you start each day with intention, reflection, and creativity. With five engaging topics, you'll have the opportunity to explore your feelings, express your thoughts, and develop essential social-emotional skills. Each activity is crafted to promote self-awareness, encourage communication, and foster creativity in a fun and interactive way. Here's a quick preview of what's inside:

1. About Me

Discover who you are and what makes you unique! This topic invites you to reflect on your personal qualities, interests, and experiences. Have fun sharing details about yourself that make you feel proud and embrace your individuality.

2. Feelings and Things

Emotions are powerful! This topic helps you explore your feelings, both big and small. By understanding your emotions and thoughts, you'll be able to respond to situations with greater confidence and self-awareness.

3. Would You Rather

This topic is all about expressing your likes, dislikes, and personal choices. Through fun and thoughtful "Would You Rather" questions, you will have a chance to share your opinions and discover new perspectives.

4. Create

Let your imagination run wild! For this topic, you will have the opportunity to design and create. Whether it is drawing, building, or writing, your creations are a reflection of your unique ideas and creativity.

5. Life Comics and Add To

Unleash your inner storyteller! Use these two topics to create comics that reflect real-life experiences or add your ideas to an existing story. It's a great way to express your creativity while practicing narrative skills and exploring how stories unfold.

© MOODAMALS

About Me

Draw a Picture of Yourself.

Feelings & Things

What Do You Want Your Teacher to Know About You?

Would You Rather

Work by Yourself or Work with Others?

_____

_____

_____

_____

_____

_____

_____

_____

_____

_____

Create

Color the Picture.

Life Comics

What Are Some of Your Favorite Things?

About Me

Draw a Picture of Your Family.

Feelings & Things

What Is Something You Like to Do with Your Family?

Would You Rather

Play with a Lot of People or Play with One Person?

_____

_____

_____

_____

_____

_____

_____

_____

_____

Create

a Bicycle on the Wheels.

Life Comics

What Is a Fun Trip You Went on with Your Family?

About Me

Draw a Picture of Your Favorite Food.

Feelings & Things

What Are Some of Your Hobbies?

Would You Rather

Eat Pizza or Spaghetti for Your Whole Life?

_____

_____

_____

_____

_____

_____

_____

_____

_____

Create

Design Your Chip Bag.

Life Comics

How Do You Make Your Favorite Food?

About Me

Draw a Picture of Your Favorite Toy or Game.

Feelings & Things

Draw a Picture Using
Your Favorite Color.

Would You Rather

Play Video Games or Board Games?

_____

_____

_____

_____

_____

_____

_____

_____

_____

_____

Create

a Game Piece for a New Board Game in the Box Below.

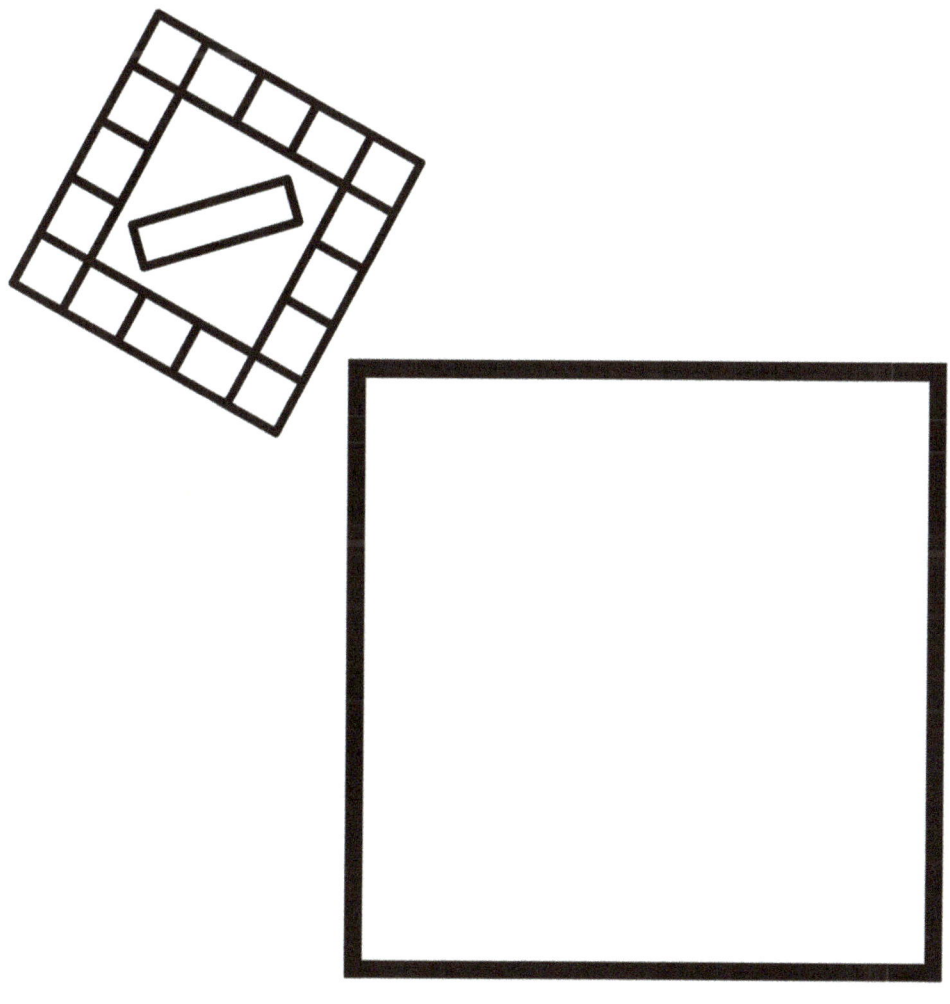

My Board Game Piece

Life Comics

Create the Steps to Play Your Favorite Game.

About Me

Draw a Picture of
Your Favorite Animal.

Feelings & Things

Draw a Picture of You with Your Favorite Animal.

Would You Rather

Live in the Ocean or
Fly in the Sky?

_____
_____
_____
_____
_____
_____
_____
_____
_____
_____

Create

a Habitat for Your Favorite Animal.

Life Comics

Draw a Journey Your Favorite Animal Went On.

About Me

Draw a Picture of You with Your Best Friend.

Feelings & Things

Draw Something You and Your Best Friend Have in Common.

Would You Rather

Have One Great Friend or Be Popular with No Close Friends?

_____

_____

_____

_____

_____

_____

_____

_____

_____

_____

Create

Color the Picture.

Life Comics

Draw Something You Love to Do with Your Best Friend.

About Me

Draw a Picture of Your Favorite Movie.

Feelings & Things

What Is Something You Are Really Great at Doing?

Would You Rather

Act in a Movie or Design the Set for Actors?

_____
_____
_____
_____
_____
_____
_____
_____
_____
_____

Create

a Bucket for the Popcorn to Go in.

Life Comics

Create a Scene from Your Favorite Movie on the Screen.

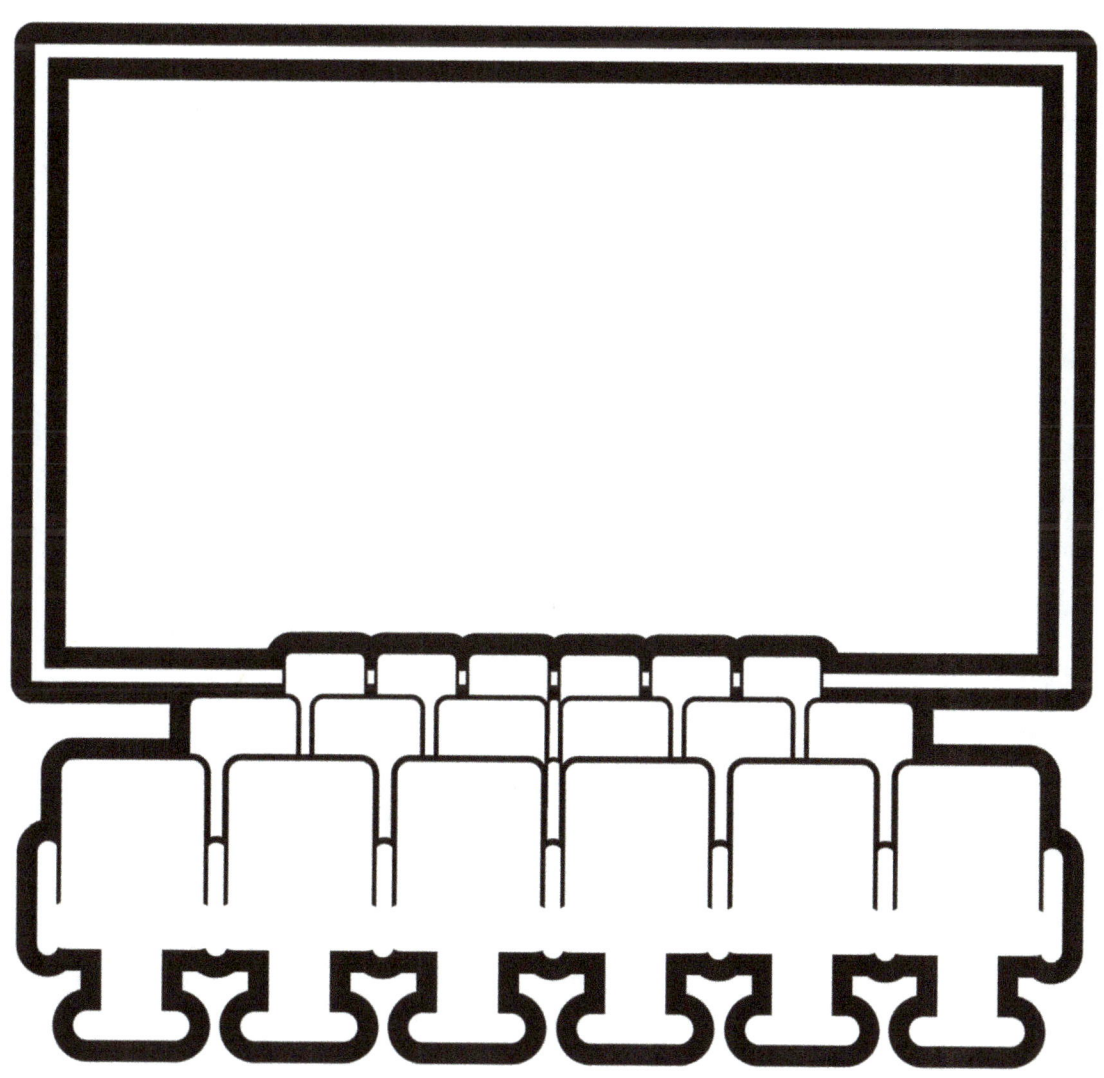

About Me

Draw a Picture of a Character in Your Favorite Book.

Feelings & Things

Draw Something That Is Important to You.

Would You Rather

Never Read a Book or Never Watch a Movie?

_____

_____

_____

_____

_____

_____

_____

_____

_____

Create

a Cover for Your Favorite Book.

Life Comics

Show What Happens in Your Favorite Book.

About Me

Draw a Picture of Your Favorite Place to Visit.

Feelings & Things

What Is Something That Makes You Feel Adventurous?

Would You Rather

Ride in a Car or
Take a Plane on a Trip?

_____

_____

_____

_____

_____

_____

_____

_____

_____

_____

Create

a Billboard Ad for a New Place to Visit.

Life Comics

Show What Happens at Your Favorite Place to Visit.

About Me

Draw a Picture of or Write the Lyrics of Your Favorite Song.

Feelings & Things

Draw Some Things That
Make You Feel Happy.

Would You Rather

Sing a Song or Write the Lyrics of a Song?

_____

_____

_____

_____

_____

_____

_____

_____

_____

_____

Create

a Singer for the Stage.

Life Comics

Create the Story of Your Favorite Song.

About Me

Draw a Picture of Your Favorite Ice Cream Flavor.

Feelings & Things

What Makes You Feel Excited?

Would You Rather

Eat Chocolate or Vanilla Ice Cream?

_____

_____

_____

_____

_____

_____

_____

_____

_____

_____

Create

Color the Ice Cream and Add Toppings.

Life Comics

Draw the Steps to Make an Ice Cream Cone.

About Me

Draw a Picture of Your Favorite Drink.

Feelings & Things

Draw Some Things That
Make You Feel Silly.

Would You Rather

Drink Soda or Sweet Tea?

_____

_____

_____

_____

_____

_____

_____

_____

_____

_____

Create

Color Your Cup and Give It a Fancy Straw.

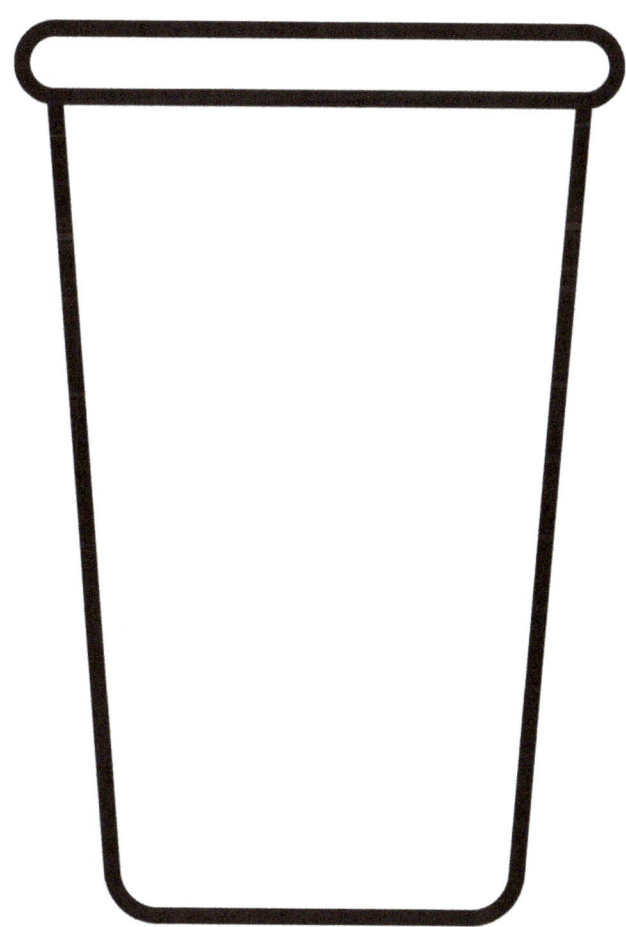

Life Comics

Create an Adventure That Includes Your Favorite Drink.

About Me

Draw a Picture of Your Favorite Sea Animal.

Feelings & Things
What Makes You Feel Calm?

Would You Rather

Be a Shark or a Dolphin?

_____

_____

_____

_____

_____

_____

_____

_____

_____

_____

Create

Color the Picture.

Life Comics

Create an Underwater Story.

About Me

Draw a Picture of Your Favorite Land Animal.

Feelings & Things

What Makes You Feel Angry?

Would You Rather

Be Able to Fly or
Be the Fastest Animal?

_____

_____

_____

_____

_____

_____

_____

_____

_____

Create

the Home of Your Favorite Animal.

Life Comics

Take Your Favorite Animal on an Adventure.

About Me

Draw a Picture of Your Room.

Feelings & Things
What Makes You Feel Shy?

Would You Rather

Have a Big Room with 5 Toys or a Small Room with 50 Toys?

_____

_____

_____

_____

_____

_____

_____

_____

_____

_____

Create

a Piece of Art for Your Room on the Canvas Below.

Life Comics

Rooms in Your Dream Home.

About Me

Draw a Picture of a Loaded Taco.

Feelings & Things

Draw Something That Makes You Feel Sad.

Would You Rather

Eat Pizza or Tacos?

_____

_____

_____

_____

_____

_____

_____

_____

_____

_____

Create

Your Most Favorite Pizza.

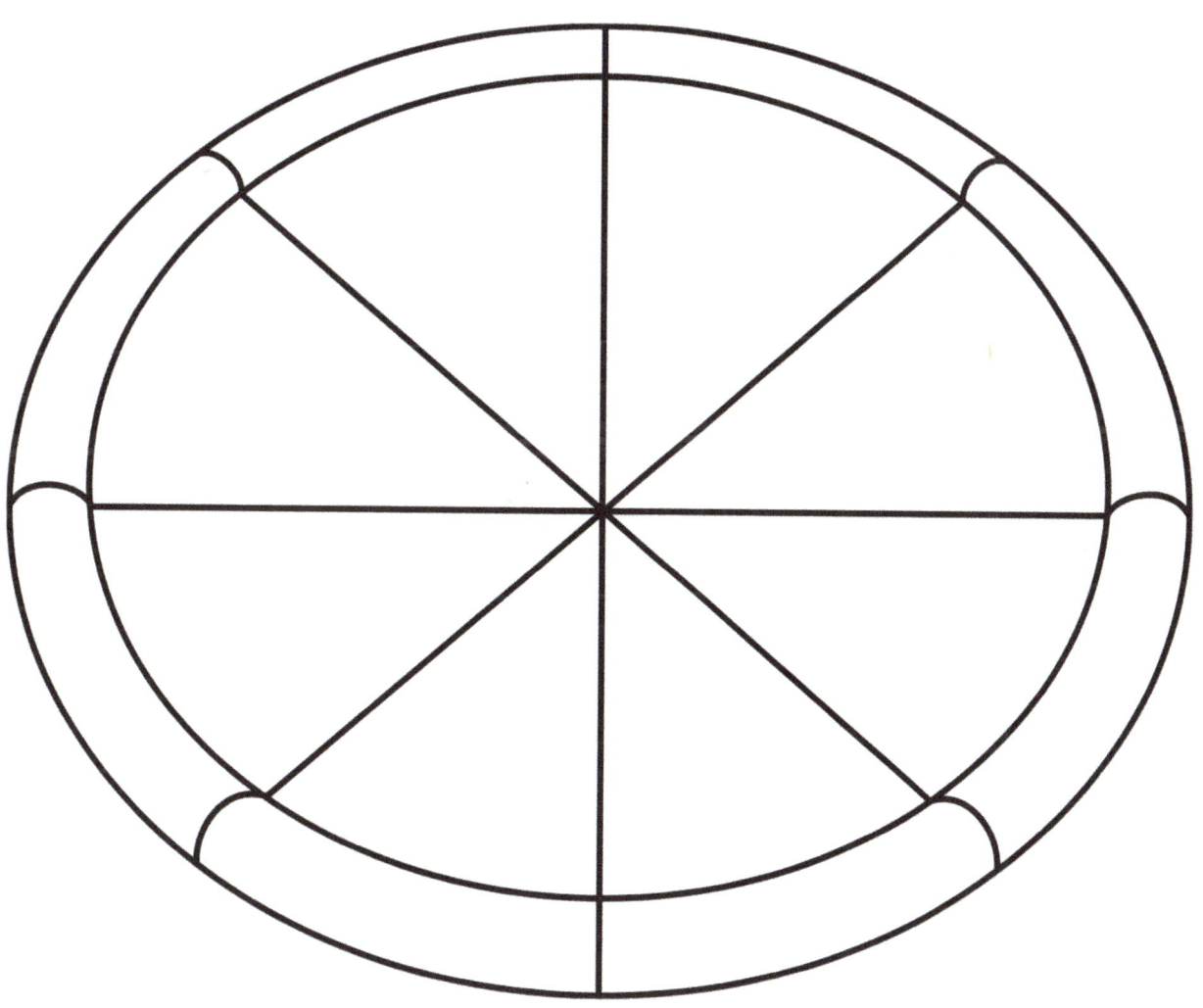

Life Comics

Draw the Steps for Building a Pizza.

About Me

Draw a Picture of Your Favorite Sports Team.

Feelings & Things

What Is Something That Makes You Feel Brave?

Would You Rather

Be Brave or Loyal?

_____

_____

_____

_____

_____

_____

_____

_____

_____

_____

Create

Design a New Hat for Your Favorite Team.

Life Comics

Draw Your Favorite Sports Team Playing a Game.

About Me

Draw a Picture of Your Favorite Video Game.

Feelings & Things

Draw Something That
Makes You Feel Worried.

Would You Rather

Never Play Video Games or Never Play Outside?

_____
_____
_____
_____
_____
_____
_____
_____
_____
_____

Create

a New Controller for Your Video Game.

Life Comics

Create Ideas for Your Own Video Game.

About Me

Draw a Picture of
a Goal You Have.

Feelings & Things

Draw a Path Leading to Your Goal; Add Advantages and Obstacles Along the Way.

Would You Rather

Fail Doing Something You Love or Succeed at Something You Don't Like?

_____

_____

_____

_____

_____

_____

_____

_____

_____

_____

Create
a Picture of You Reaching Your Goal.

Add To
the Sky.

About Me

Draw a Picture of Your Favorite Sport to Play.

Feelings & Things

Draw Something That Makes You Feel Creative.

Would You Rather

Be the Best Player on the Worst Team or the Worst Player on the Best Team?

_____

_____

_____

_____

_____

_____

_____

_____

_____

Create

Draw a Design on the Trophy.

Add To

Create Art on Your Shirt.

About Me

Draw Your Favorite Number in Different Colors.

Feelings & Things

What Does Kindness Mean to You?

Would You Rather

Make *Your* Dreams Come True or the Dreams of *Others*?

_____

_____

_____

_____

_____

_____

_____

_____

_____

Create

Color the Picture.

Add To
the Group of Balloons.

About Me

Draw Different Sizes of Your Favorite Shape.

Feelings & Things

What Does Creativity Mean to You?

Would You Rather

Be Very Creative or Be Very Smart?

_____

_____

_____

_____

_____

_____

_____

_____

_____

_____

Create

a Picture Using Your Favorite Shapes.

Add To
the Shape Design.

About Me

Draw a Picture of Your Favorite Breakfast.

Feelings & Things

What Does Pride Mean to You?

Would You Rather

Eat Waffles or Bacon and Eggs?

_____

_____

_____

_____

_____

_____

_____

_____

_____

Create

a Picture of Something You Are Proud of.

Add To
the Dinner Plate.

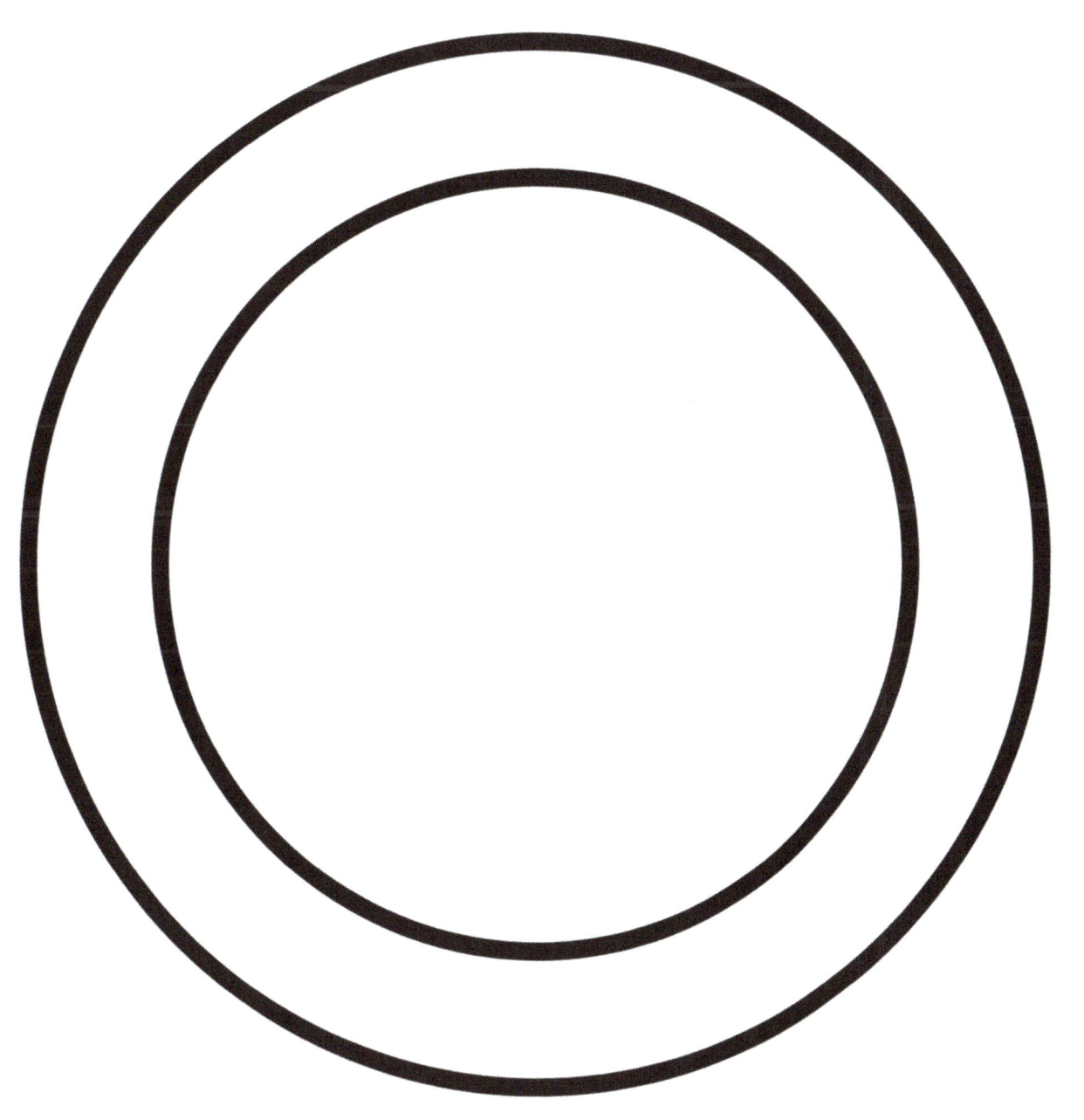

About Me

Draw a Picture of Yourself in Your Favorite Outfit or Hat.

Feelings & Things
What Does Funny Mean to You?

Would You Rather

Wear Nice Clothes or Have Nice Things?

___
___
___
___
___
___
___
___
___
___

Create

Draw a Picture of Something Funny.

Add To
the Designs on the Backpack.

About Me

Draw a Picture of Your Favorite Carnival Ride.

Feelings & Things

What Does Adventure Mean to You?

Would You Rather

Go on a Roller Coaster or a Waterslide Ride?

_____

_____

_____

_____

_____

_____

_____

_____

_____

_____

Create

a Background for the Monster.

Add To
the Carnival.

About Me

Draw a Picture of Your Favorite Chocolate Bar.

Feelings & Things
What Does Love Mean to You?

Would You Rather

Eat Chocolate or Potato Chips?

_____

_____

_____

_____

_____

_____

_____

_____

_____

_____

Create

a House Made of Cookies and Chips.

Add To
the Lollipop Garden.

About Me

Draw a Picture of You in Your Favorite Costume.

Feelings & Things

What Does Bravery Mean to You?

Would You Rather

Read About a Hero or Villain in a Story?

_____

_____

_____

_____

_____

_____

_____

_____

_____

_____

Create

a Villain or a Superhero Coming Out of the Light.

Add To
the Superhero Cape.

About Me

Draw a Picture of Your Home.

Feelings & Things

What Does Family Mean to You?

Would You Rather

Share Your Room with a Dinosaur or a Dragon?

_____

_____

_____

_____

_____

_____

_____

_____

_____

_____

Create

a Picture of Your Dream House.

Add To
the Roof of the House.

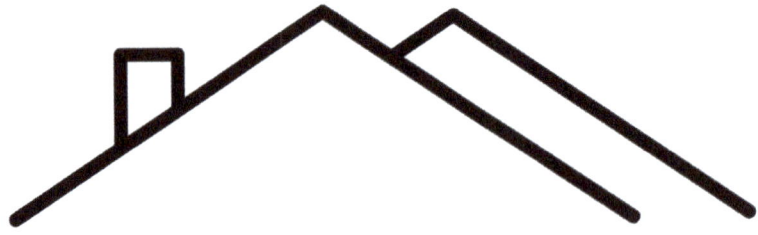

About Me

Draw a Picture of Your Favorite Outdoor Space.

Feelings & Things

What Does Nature Mean to You?

Would You Rather

Be at the Beach or
in the Woods?

_____

_____

_____

_____

_____

_____

_____

_____

_____

_____

Create

Color the Picture.

Add To

Draw a Treehouse for the Tree.

About Me

Draw a Picture of What You Like to Draw the Most.

Feelings & Things

What Does Calm Look Like to You?

Would You Rather

Give Up Social Media or Give Up Your Favorite Food?

_____

_____

_____

_____

_____

_____

_____

_____

_____

Create

a Favorite Things List.

- _____
- _____
- _____
- _____
- _____
- _____
- _____

Add To

a World of Bubbles.

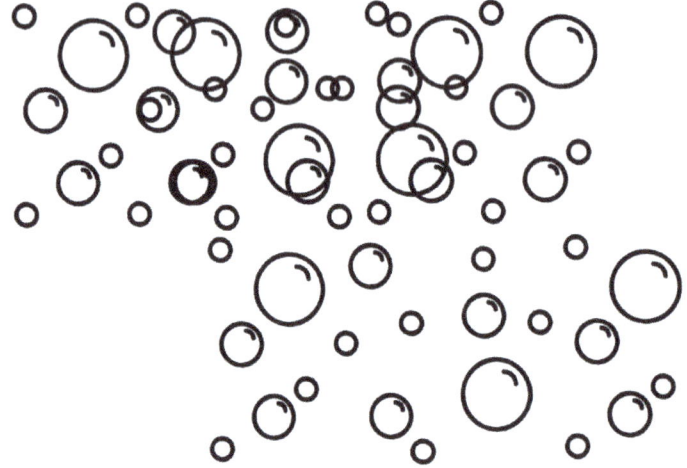

About Me

Draw a Picture of Your Favorite Person.

Feelings & Things

Draw Adventures to Go on with Your Favorite Person

Would You Rather

Have a Swimming Pool or a Trampoline?

_____

_____

_____

_____

_____

_____

_____

_____

_____

_____

Create
a New Beach Ball Design.

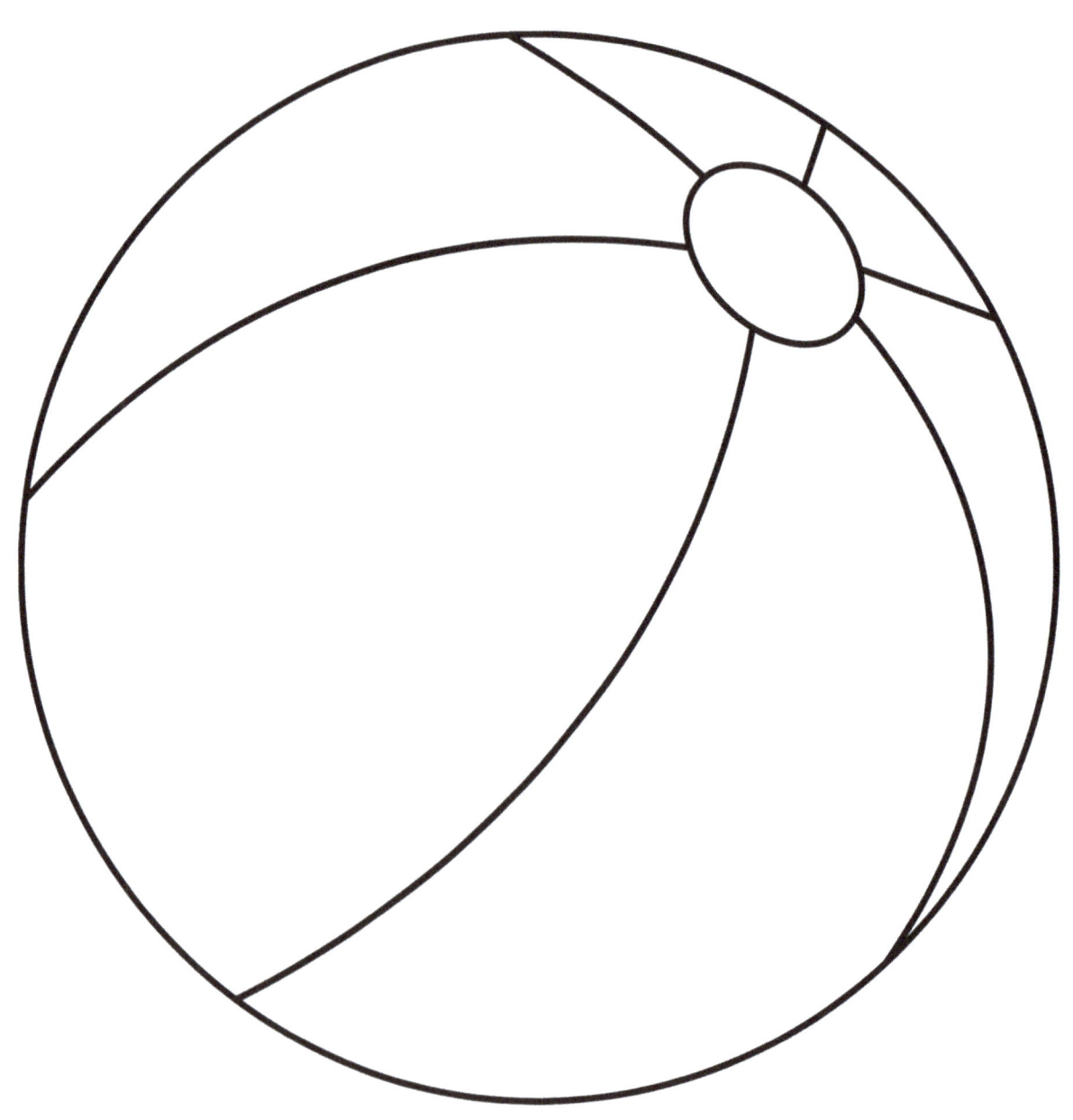

Add To
a World of Emojis.

About Me

Draw a Picture of Your Favorite Chips.

Feelings & Things

Draw a Time When You Told the Truth, Then Worried About the Outcome.

Would You Rather

Have a Pet Snake or a Pet Rat?

_____

_____

_____

_____

_____

_____

_____

_____

_____

_____

Create
a Playground for the Snake.

Add To
a World of Candy.

About Me

Draw a Picture of You Celebrating on Your Favorite Holiday.

Feelings & Things
What Does It Mean to Be Silly?

Would You Rather

Live on the Moon or
Live in the Ocean?

_____

_____

_____

_____

_____

_____

_____

_____

_____

_____

Create

a Background of Stars.

Add To

a World of Blocks.

About Me

Draw a Picture of You on Your Favorite Day.

Feelings & Things

Draw a Time When You Felt Silly.

Would You Rather

Drink Soda or Juice?

_____

_____

_____

_____

_____

_____

_____

_____

_____

_____

Create
a Mushroom Garden.

Add To
a World of Waterslides.

About Me

Draw a Picture of Your Favorite Candy.

Feelings & Things

What Does It Mean to Be a Good Friend?

Would You Rather

Be a Dog or a Cat?

_____

_____

_____

_____

_____

_____

_____

_____

_____

_____

Create

a Bed for the Cat.

Add To
a World of Balloons.

About Me

Draw a Picture of Something You Love the Most.

Feelings & Things

Draw a Time When You Were a Good Friend to Someone.

Would You Rather

Never Watch Another Movie or Never Hear Another Song?

_____

_____

_____

_____

_____

_____

_____

_____

_____

Create

a Movie Background for Your Tickets.

Add To
a World of Ice Cream.

About the Author

Sheila Garth is an educator and a certified Arts Integration Specialist with a master's in school counseling and a bachelor's in journalism. She is passionate about fostering student growth and has dedicated her career to supporting student academic, social, and emotional development through innovative and creative approaches. Sheila currently resides in Charleston, South Carolina with her husband Jimmy and their two children Lylah and James. When not inspiring young minds, she enjoys photography, writing, traveling, and spending time at the beach.

www.ingramcontent.com/pod-product-compliance
Lightning Source LLC
Chambersburg PA
CBHW080549030426
42337CB00024B/4815